Kenlyn's Reading Expedition Operation:

Learn to Read!

Written by
Alisa L. Grace

© 2024 Alisa L. Grace
All rights reserved.

No part of this book may be reproduced in any form or by any electronic or mechanical means, including information storage and retrieval systems, without permission in writing from the publisher.

Self-Published by
Alisa L. Grace
Sanford, FL 32771

ISBN: 978-1-966129-19-6

First Edition

Printed in the United States of America

Library of Congress Cataloging-in-Publication Data
Grace, Alisa L.
Title of the Book: Kenlyn's Reading Expedition Operation: Learn to Read!
Library of Congress Control Number:2024923782

Disclaimer: The views expressed in this book are those of the author and do not necessarily reflect any organizations or individuals mentioned.

Acknowledgments: The author wishes to thank God, Her Husband (Linion), Victory Temple of God, Florida SPECS, Unity Youth Association, All About Serving You, Angels-ANJ Events, NordeVest, and Love & Create Life for their support and contributions.

Dearest Kenlyn,

Welcome to your very own reading adventure! This book is a special gift made just for you. Inside these pages, you'll discover a world of words, just waiting to be explored. We'll visit the zoo and meet amazing animals, hike through nature trails, and even learn how to cook up some tasty treats with Mom! Reading is like having a superpower – it can take you anywhere you want to go and teach you all sorts of incredible things. So, cuddle up with your family, turn the page, and get ready to unlock the magic of reading!

With lots of love,
NeNe

Table of Contents

Chapter 1: Reading at Home on Base 9

Chapter 2: Reading Adventures Around the Base 17

Chapter 3: Animal Adventures at the NC Zoo 23

Chapter 4: Discovering Nature and History 31

Chapter 5: Reading with Technology and Family 39

Chapter 1: Reading at Home on Base

Chapter 1:
Reading at Home on Base

Story:

Kenlyn loved story time with her family. They would snuggle on the couch in their cozy living room on base every night. Dad would read exciting tales of brave soldiers and faraway lands in his uniform. Mom would tell funny stories about playful puppies and mischievous kittens. Noah, her big brother, would make silly voices for each character, making Kenlyn giggle.

One day, while looking at a book about a chameleon changing colors, Kenlyn wanted to read the words herself. "I want to read about the chameleon!" she declared. Mom smiled. "That's a wonderful idea, Kenlyn! We can learn together." And so, with her family's help, Kenlyn started her reading adventure, discovering the magic hidden in every word and every page.

Activity (10 minutes):

- **Camouflage Alphabet Hunt:** Hide letter cards (uppercase and lowercase) decorated with camouflage patterns around the room. Have Kenlyn search for the letters and match them to a corresponding alphabet chart. As she finds each letter, have her sound it out and try to find an object that starts with that letter in the room.

Reading with Noah is fun!

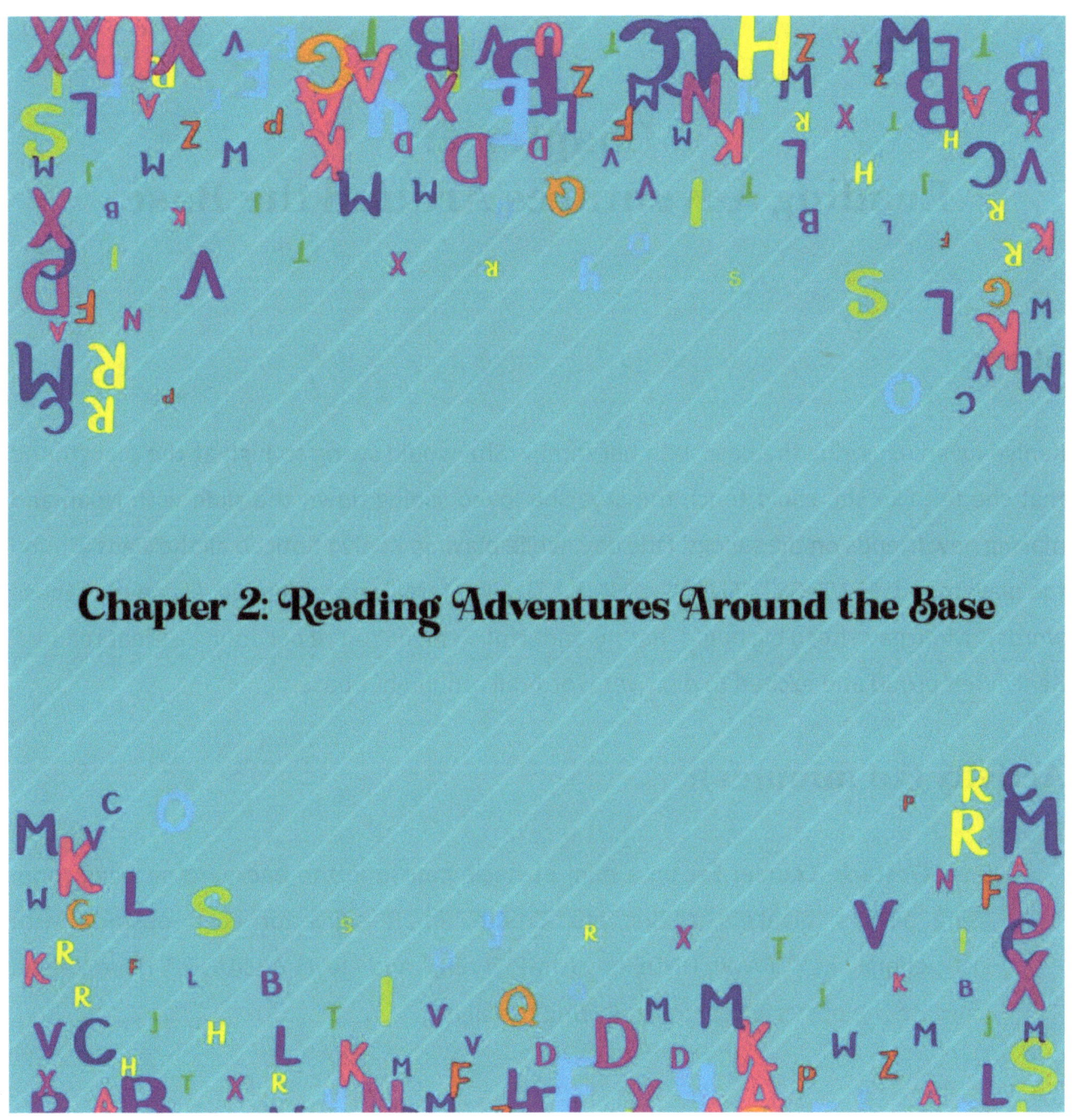

Chapter 2: Reading Adventures Around the Base

Chapter 2:
Reading Adventures Around the Base

Story:

Kenlyn loved exploring the base with her family. She would swing so high at the playground that she felt like she could touch the sky! She loved sliding down the slide with Noah and making new friends on the swings. One day, while playing, Kenlyn noticed all the signs around the playground: "SWINGS," "SLIDE," "CLIMB." "Look, Mom!" she exclaimed, "I can read those words!" Mom gave her a big hug. "That's wonderful, Kenlyn! You're becoming a great reader." Kenlyn felt proud and excited to discover words all around her base.

Activity (10 minutes):

- **Base Obstacle Course:** Set up a mini obstacle course in the backyard or living room using pillows, blankets, chairs, etc. Create simple signs for each obstacle with instructions like "CRAWL UNDER," "JUMP OVER," and "RUN AROUND." Have Kenlyn navigate the obstacle course by reading the signs.

Chapter 3: Animal Adventures at the NC Zoo

Chapter 3:
Animal Adventures at the NC Zoo

Story:

The NC Zoo was Kenlyn's favorite place! She loved seeing all the amazing animals, especially the playful penguins and the roaring tigers. Walking through the zoo with her family, she noticed signs with the animals' names and fun facts about them. "Wow, Dad!" she exclaimed, "This sign says the giraffe is the tallest mammal!" Dad smiled. "That's right, Kenlyn! You're learning so much by reading." Kenlyn felt like she was on a real-life animal adventure, and reading made it even more exciting.

Activity (10 minutes):

- **Animal Charades:** Write the names of different animals on slips of paper. Have each family member act out an animal while the others guess. Encourage Kenlyn to read the animal's name aloud once it's been guessed.

Welcome to the zoo!

The elephants use their TRUNKS!

Chapter 4: Discovering Nature and History

Chapter 4:
Discovering Nature and History

Story:

One sunny morning, Kenlyn and her family went on a nature hike. They followed a winding trail, listening to the birds chirping and the leaves rustling. Kenlyn loved looking for animal tracks and collecting colorful leaves. Along the trail, they found a sign that said, "NATURE TRAIL." "I can read that!" Kenlyn shouted, jumping up and down. Later that day, they visited a museum filled with old artifacts and stories about North Carolina's history. Kenlyn was fascinated by the exhibits and loved learning about the past.

Activity (10 minutes):

- **Nature Scavenger Hunt:** Create a list of simple nature items for Kenlyn to find on a walk around the neighborhood or a local park (e.g., a feather, a pinecone, a smooth rock). Write the list using simple words and have Kenlyn check off each item as she finds it.

Hiking on a nature trail!

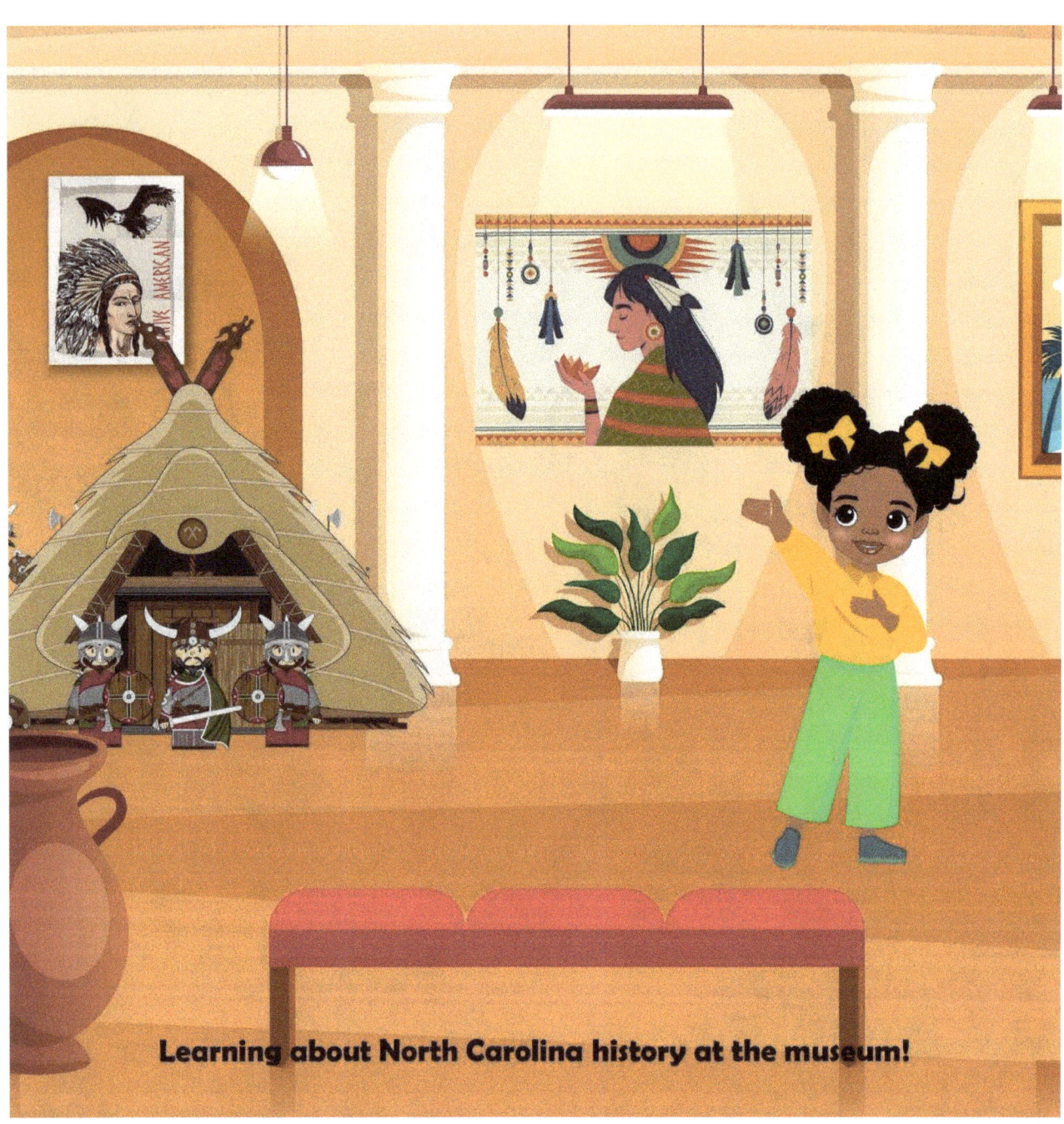

Learning about North Carolina history at the museum!

Visiting a historic fort!

Sharing what we learned!

Chapter 5: Reading with Technology and Family

Chapter 5:
Reading with Technology and Family

Story:

Kenlyn loved using her Amazon Fire tablet to watch videos about her favorite animals and play learning games. One day, she discovered an app with stories about playful puppies and adventurous kittens. She loved reading the stories on her tablet and listening to the words being read aloud. After her reading session, she used the tablet to video chat with Grandma and showed her all the new words she had learned. Grandma was so proud of Kenlyn's reading progress!

Activity (10 minutes):

- **Digital Storytelling:** Take pictures of Kenlyn's favorite toys or objects around the house using a tablet or phone. Then, have her create a simple story using the images and dictate it to a family member to write down. You can even use a drawing app to let her illustrate her story.

Reading animal stories on my Amazon Fire tablet!

Watching videos about animals!

Video chatting with Grandma and sharing our animal book!

Meet the Author of Kenlyn's Reading Expedition: Operation Learn to Read!

Alisa Ladawn Grace is a retired school administrator, Chief Operating Officer of a nonprofit organization, Transformation Life Coach, and a passionate advocate for empowering children through education. With a Specialist Degree in Curriculum and Instruction, Alisa has dedicated her life to creating impactful educational experiences for young learners. Her deep expertise in education and her love for teaching allow her to develop creative and engaging content that supports children's academic and personal growth.

In her latest children's book, *Kenlyn's Reading Expedition: Operation Learn to Read!*, Alisa uses her extensive experience to craft an exciting reading journey for young children. The book aims to spark a love for reading, encouraging children to explore the joys of learning while developing essential literacy skills. Alisa believes that reading opens doors to imagination, knowledge, and lifelong success.

In addition to her work in literacy, Alisa is the author of the practical guide *Unlocking Your Great Potential Within You: The Supernatural Powers of Meditation, Executive Functioning Skills, and Good Habits for Kids 3-18 Years Old.* This guide is not just a book but a toolkit for success and well-being. It equips children with tools they can apply immediately, emphasizing the importance of faith, integrity, and love in a way that's practical and accessible.

Through her writing, Alisa seeks to make a lasting, positive impact on the lives of children and families, nurturing their intellectual and emotional development. Her passion for education and mission to foster a lifelong love for learning and civic engagement are evident in everything she does, unlocking the great potential of every young reader and citizen.

Join Kenlyn on a magical reading adventure! This curious little girl loves animals, cooking, and exploring her world on base with her family. With a sprinkle of fun and a dash of determination, she's ready to discover the magic of words. This book will have young readers giggling and learning along with Kenlyn as she explores the zoo, hikes nature trails, and even creates her own stories. Get ready to turn the page and embark on an unforgettable reading expedition!

www.ingramcontent.com/pod-product-compliance
Lightning Source LLC
Chambersburg PA
CBHW050456110426
42743CB00017B/3391